TO DO JUSTICE TO LOVE KINDNESS TO WALK HUMBLY

for kids

A STUDY ON MICAH

LOVEGODGREATLY.COM

TO DO JUSTICE, TO LOVE KINDNESS, TO WALK HUMBLY: A STUDY ON MICAH

Published in Dallas by Love God Greatly.

Photos from unsplash.com

Printed in the United States of America

Library of Congress Cataloging-in-Publication Data

Printed in the United States of America

24 23 22 21 20 19

6 5 4 3 2 1

A Word to Parents

This book grew out of a desire to provide a companion study journal for children to use alongside the *To Do Justice, to Love Kindness, to Walk Humbly: A study on Micah* adult study journal and book.

Love God Greatly is dedicated to making God's Word available to our beautiful community of women... and now, women have the opportunity to share God's Word with children through this study uniquely crafted for young hearts.

CONTENTS

INTRODUCTION

TO DO JUSTICE, TO LOVE KINDNESS, TO WALK HUMBLY

Hey friend,

We are so excited you are joining us for this four-week study in the book of Micah! We don't know a lot about the prophet Micah, except that he lived around the same time as Isaiah and Hosea. But nevertheless, God gave Micah a very important message to tell the people of Israel, a message that is even for you and me! How amazing is that?!

A lot of people were making unwise and selfish decisions in Micah's day. They were living to make themselves happy instead of living their lives out of love for God. Sure, at times they acted like they loved God...but their hearts were far from Him. Plus, they were involved in idolatry. Idolatry is a fancy word for loving something more than God. When we do, that person or thing becomes an idol in our lives and not only does that dishonor God, but it makes Him sad, too.

In Hosea 6:6 we are told that God wants our hearts, not our sacrifices. That means God wants us to love Him, not just go through the motions of obeying God and acting like we love Him. He wants us to obey Him **because** we love Him. What an important lesson to learn early in life!

The people in Micah's time were struggling with many sins that kids and adults struggle with today. Sins like greed, stealing from others, and even violence.

Over the next four weeks, you will learn in this very important book that God gives both judgment and forgiveness. Judgment happens when we've done something sinful, something that is hurtful to others, to ourselves or to God. Because God is good and Holy, there are consequences for our sins. But the prophet Micah also reminds us that we serve a God who is loving, kind and willing to forgive us. Sweet one, always remember that God loves you. He is rich in mercy and slow to get angry. He hates sin but loves the sinner. Never forget that truth.

Our prayer is that you will grow stronger in our faith as you read the book of Micah and live lives that "do justice, love kindness and walk humbly with Him." Micah 6:8

Cheering you on!

READING PLAN

WEEK 1

Monday
Read: Micah 1:1, 2 Chronicles 27:1-2; 28:1-4; 29:1-2
SOAP: 2 Chronicles 29:2
For Further Reading: 2 Chronicles 27-28

Tuesday
Read: Micah 1:2-7, 2 Kings 17:7-13
SOAP: Micah 1:2-3
For Further Reading: 2 Chronicles 29

Wednesday
Read: Micah 1:8-16, 2 Kings 17:14-23
SOAP: 2 Kings 17:18-20

Thursday
Read: Micah 2:1-5, 2 Chronicles 36:15-21
SOAP: 2 Chronicles 36:15

Friday
Read: Micah 2:6-11, Deuteronomy 11:13-17
SOAP: Micah 2:7

WEEK 2

Monday
Read: Micah 2:12-13, Psalm 103:1-14
SOAP: Micah 2:12

Tuesday
Read: Micah 3:1-4, Isaiah 55:8-9
SOAP: Isaiah 55:8-9

Wednesday
Read: Micah 3:5-8, James 5:19-20
SOAP: Micah 3:8

Thursday
Read: Micah 3:9-12, Psalm 82
SOAP: Psalm 82:8

Friday
Read: Micah 4:1-5, Revelation 21:1-8
SOAP: Micah 4:5

WEEK 3

Monday
Read: Micah 4:6-8, Psalm 93
SOAP: Micah 4:7

Tuesday
Read: Micah 4:9-13, Romans 8:28
SOAP: Micah 4:12

Wednesday
Read: Micah 5:1-6, 2 Chronicles 32:20-23
SOAP: Micah 5:4-5a
For Further Reading: 2 Chronicles 32

Thursday
Read: Micah 5:7-9, Acts 17:1-4; 18:1-4, 24
SOAP: Micah 5:7
For Further Reading: Acts 17, 18, 19

Friday
Read: Micah 5:10-15, Psalm 50:15-23
SOAP: Micah 5:15

WEEK 4

Monday
Read: Micah 6:1-8, Galatians 4:12-16
SOAP: Micah 6:8

Tuesday
Read: Micah 6:9-15, Job 40:1-9
SOAP: Job 40:8-9

Wednesday
Read: Micah 7:1-7
SOAP: Micah 7:7

Thursday
Read: Micah 7:8-13
SOAP: Micah 7:8-9

Friday
Read: Micah 7:14-20
SOAP: Micah 7:18-20

YOUR GOALS

We believe it's important to write out goals for this study. Take some time now and write three goals you would like to focus on as you begin to rise each day and dig into God's Word. Make sure and refer back to these goals throughout the next weeks to help you stay focused. You can do it!

1.

2.

3.

Signature:

Date:

PRAYER

WRITE DOWN YOUR PRAYER REQUESTS AND PRAISES FOR EACH DAY.

Prayer focus for this week:
Spend time praying for your family members.

MONDAY

TUESDAY

WEDNESDAY

THURSDAY

FRIDAY

WEEK 1

Should this be said,
O house of Jacob?
Has the Lord grown impatient?
Are these his deeds?
Do not my words do good
to him who walks uprightly?

Micah 2:7

SCRIPTURE FOR WEEK 1

MONDAY

Micah 1:1

1 The word of the Lord that came to Micah of Moresheth in the days of Jotham, Ahaz, and Hezekiah, kings of Judah, which he saw concerning Samaria and Jerusalem.

2 Chronicles 27:1-2

1 Jotham was twenty-five years old when he began to reign, and he reigned sixteen years in Jerusalem. His mother's name was Jerushah the daughter of Zadok. 2 And he did what was right in the eyes of the Lord according to all that his father Uzziah had done, except he did not enter the temple of the Lord. But the people still followed corrupt practices.

2 Chronicles 28:1-4

1 Ahaz was twenty years old when he began to reign, and he reigned sixteen years in Jerusalem. And he did not do what was right in the eyes of the Lord, as his father David had done, 2 but he walked in the ways of the kings of Israel. He even made metal images for the Baals, 3 and he made offerings in the Valley of the Son of Hinnom and burned his sons as an offering, according to the abominations of the nations whom the Lord drove out before the people of Israel.4 And he sacrificed and made offerings on the high places and on the hills and under every green tree.

2 Chronicles 29:1-2

1 Hezekiah began to reign when he was twenty-five years old, and he reigned twenty-nine years in Jerusalem. His mother's name was Abijah the daughter of Zechariah. 2 And he did what was right in the eyes of the Lord, according to all that David his father had done.

For Further Reading: 2 Chronicles 27-28

TUESDAY

Micah 1:2-7

2 Hear, you peoples, all of you;
pay attention, O earth, and all that is in it,
and let the Lord God be a witness against you,
the Lord from his holy temple.
3 For behold, the Lord is coming out of his place,
and will come down and tread upon the high places of the earth.
4 And the mountains will melt under him,
and the valleys will split open,
like wax before the fire,

like waters poured down a steep place.
5 All this is for the transgression of Jacob
and for the sins of the house of Israel.
What is the transgression of Jacob?
Is it not Samaria?
And what is the high place of Judah?
Is it not Jerusalem?
6 Therefore I will make Samaria a heap in the open country,
a place for planting vineyards,
and I will pour down her stones into the valley
and uncover her foundations.
7 All her carved images shall be beaten to pieces,
all her wages shall be burned with fire,
and all her idols I will lay waste,
for from the fee of a prostitute she gathered them,
and to the fee of a prostitute they shall return.

2 Kings 17:7-13

7 And this occurred because the people of Israel had sinned against the Lord their God, who had brought them up out of the land of Egypt from under the hand of Pharaoh king of Egypt, and had feared other gods 8 and walked in the customs of the nations whom the Lord drove out before the people of Israel, and in the customs that the kings of Israel had practiced. 9 And the people of Israel did secretly against the Lord their God things that were not right. They built for themselves high places in all their towns, from watchtower to fortified city. 10 They set up for themselves pillars and Asherim on every high hill and under every green tree, 11 and there they made offerings on all the high places, as the nations did whom the Lord carried away before them. And they did wicked things, provoking the Lord to anger, 12 and they served idols, of which the Lord had said to them, "You shall not do this." 13 Yet the Lord warned Israel and Judah by every prophet and every seer, saying, "Turn from your evil ways and keep my commandments and my statutes, in accordance with all the Law that I commanded your fathers, and that I sent to you by my servants the prophets."

For Further Reading: 2 Chronicles 29

WEDNESDAY

Micah 1:8-16

8 For this I will lament and wail;
I will go stripped and naked;
I will make lamentation like the jackals,
and mourning like the ostriches.
9 For her wound is incurable,
and it has come to Judah;
it has reached to the gate of my people,
to Jerusalem.

10 Tell it not in Gath;
   weep not at all;
in Beth-le-aphrah
   roll yourselves in the dust.
11 Pass on your way,
   inhabitants of Shaphir,
   in nakedness and shame;
the inhabitants of Zaanan
   do not come out;
the lamentation of Beth-ezel
   shall take away from you its standing place.
12 For the inhabitants of Maroth
   wait anxiously for good,
because disaster has come down from the Lord
   to the gate of Jerusalem.
13 Harness the steeds to the chariots,
   inhabitants of Lachish;
it was the beginning of sin
   to the daughter of Zion,
for in you were found
   the transgressions of Israel.
14 Therefore you shall give parting gifts
   to Moresheth-gath;
the houses of Achzib shall be a deceitful thing
   to the kings of Israel.
15 I will again bring a conqueror to you,
   inhabitants of Mareshah;
the glory of Israel
   shall come to Adullam.
16 Make yourselves bald and cut off your hair,
   for the children of your delight;
make yourselves as bald as the eagle,
   for they shall go from you into exile.

2 Kings 17:14-23

14 But they would not listen, but were stubborn, as their fathers had been, who did not believe in the Lord their God. 15 They despised his statutes and his covenant that he made with their fathers and the warnings that he gave them. They went after false idols and became false, and they followed the nations that were around them, concerning whom the Lord had commanded them that they should not do like them. 16 And they abandoned all the commandments of the Lord their God, and made for themselves metal images of two calves; and they made an Asherah and worshiped all the host of heaven and served Baal. 17 And they burned their sons and their daughters as offerings and used divination and omens and sold themselves to do evil in the sight of the Lord, provoking him to anger. 18 Therefore the Lord was very angry with Israel and removed them out of his sight. None was left but the tribe of Judah only.

19 Judah also did not keep the commandments of the Lord their God, but walked in the

customs that Israel had introduced. 20 And the Lord rejected all the descendants of Israel and afflicted them and gave them into the hand of plunderers, until he had cast them out of his sight.

21 When he had torn Israel from the house of David, they made Jeroboam the son of Nebat king. And Jeroboam drove Israel from following the Lord and made them commit great sin. 22 The people of Israel walked in all the sins that Jeroboam did. They did not depart from them, 23 until the Lord removed Israel out of his sight, as he had spoken by all his servants the prophets. So Israel was exiled from their own land to Assyria until this day.

THURSDAY

Micah 2:1-5

1 Woe to those who devise wickedness
  and work evil on their beds!
When the morning dawns, they perform it,
  because it is in the power of their hand.
2 They covet fields and seize them,
  and houses, and take them away;
they oppress a man and his house,
  a man and his inheritance.
3 Therefore thus says the Lord:
behold, against this family I am devising disaster,
  from which you cannot remove your necks,
and you shall not walk haughtily,
  for it will be a time of disaster.
4 In that day they shall take up a taunt song against you
  and moan bitterly,
and say, "We are utterly ruined;
  he changes the portion of my people;
how he removes it from me!
  To an apostate he allots our fields."
5 Therefore you will have none to cast the line by lot
  in the assembly of the Lord.

2 Chronicles 36:15-21

15 The Lord, the God of their fathers, sent persistently to them by his messengers, because he had compassion on his people and on his dwelling place. 16 But they kept mocking the messengers of God, despising his words and scoffing at his prophets, until the wrath of the Lord rose against his people, until there was no remedy.

17 Therefore he brought up against them the king of the Chaldeans, who killed their young men with the sword in the house of their sanctuary and had no compassion on young man or virgin, old man or aged. He gave them all into his hand. 18 And all the vessels of the house of God, great and small, and the treasures of the house of the Lord, and the treasures of the king and of his princes, all these he brought to Babylon. 19 And they burned the house of God and broke down the wall of Jerusalem and burned all its palaces with fire and

destroyed all its precious vessels. 20 He took into exile in Babylon those who had escaped from the sword, and they became servants to him and to his sons until the establishment of the kingdom of Persia, 21 to fulfill the word of the Lord by the mouth of Jeremiah, until the land had enjoyed its Sabbaths. All the days that it lay desolate it kept Sabbath, to fulfill seventy years.

FRIDAY

Micah 2:6-11

6 "Do not preach"—thus they preach—
"one should not preach of such things;
disgrace will not overtake us."
7 Should this be said, O house of Jacob?
Has the Lord grown impatient?
Are these his deeds?
Do not my words do good
to him who walks uprightly?
8 But lately my people have risen up as an enemy;
you strip the rich robe from those who pass by trustingly
with no thought of war.
9 The women of my people you drive out
from their delightful houses;
from their young children you take away
my splendor forever.
10 Arise and go,
for this is no place to rest,
because of uncleanness that destroys
with a grievous destruction.
11 If a man should go about and utter wind and lies,
saying, "I will preach to you of wine and strong drink,"
he would be the preacher for this people!

Deuteronomy 11:13-17

13 "And if you will indeed obey my commandments that I command you today, to love the Lord your God, and to serve him with all your heart and with all your soul,14 he will give the rain for your land in its season, the early rain and the later rain, that you may gather in your grain and your wine and your oil. 15 And he will give grass in your fields for your livestock, and you shall eat and be full. 16 Take care lest your heart be deceived, and you turn aside and serve other gods and worship them; 17 then the anger of the Lord will be kindled against you, and he will shut up the heavens, so that there will be no rain, and the land will yield no fruit, and you will perish quickly off the good land that the Lord is giving you.

MONDAY

Read:

Micah 1:1, 2 Chronicles 27:1-2; 28:1-4; 29:1-2

SOAP:

2 Chronicles 29:2

1. Write out today's **SCRIPTURE** passage.

2. On the blank page to the right, **DRAW** or **WRITE** what this passage means to you.

3. My **PRAYER** for today:

TUESDAY

Read:
Micah 1:2-7, 2 Kings 17:7-13

SOAP:
Micah 1:2-3

1. Write out today's **SCRIPTURE** passage.

2. On the blank page to the right, **DRAW** or **WRITE** what this passage means to you.

3. My **PRAYER** for today:

WEDNESDAY

Read:

Micah 1:8-16, 2 Kings 17:14-23

SOAP:

2 Kings 17:18-20

1. Write out today's **SCRIPTURE** passage.

2. On the blank page to the right, **DRAW** or **WRITE** what this passage means to you.

3. My **PRAYER** for today:

THURSDAY

Read:
Micah 2:1-5, 2 Chronicles 36:15-21

SOAP:
2 Chronicles 36:15

1. Write out today's **SCRIPTURE** passage.

2. On the blank page to the right, **DRAW** or **WRITE** what this passage means to you.

3. My **PRAYER** for today:

FRIDAY

Read:
Micah 2:6-11, Deuteronomy 11:13-17

SOAP:
Micah 2:7

1. Write out today's **SCRIPTURE** passage.

2. On the blank page to the right, **DRAW** or **WRITE** what this passage means to you.

3. My **PRAYER** for today:

THIS WEEK I LEARNED...

USE THE SPACE BELOW TO DRAW A PICTURE OR WRITE ABOUT WHAT YOU LEARNED THIS WEEK FROM YOUR TIME IN GOD'S WORD.

PRAYER

WRITE DOWN YOUR PRAYER REQUESTS AND PRAISES FOR EACH DAY.

Prayer focus for this week:
Spend time praying for your country.

MONDAY

TUESDAY

WEDNESDAY

THURSDAY

FRIDAY

WEEK 2

For all the peoples walk
each in the name of its god,
but we will walk in the
name of the Lord our God
forever and ever.

Micah 4:5

SCRIPTURE FOR WEEK 2

MONDAY

Micah 2:12-13

12 I will surely assemble all of you, O Jacob;
   I will gather the remnant of Israel;
I will set them together
   like sheep in a fold,
like a flock in its pasture,
   a noisy multitude of men.
13 He who opens the breach goes up before them;
   they break through and pass the gate,
   going out by it.
Their king passes on before them,
   the Lord at their head.

Psalm 103:1-14

1 Bless the Lord, O my soul,
   and all that is within me,
   bless his holy name!
2 Bless the Lord, O my soul,
   and forget not all his benefits,
3 who forgives all your iniquity,
   who heals all your diseases,
4 who redeems your life from the pit,
   who crowns you with steadfast love and mercy,
5 who satisfies you with good
   so that your youth is renewed like the eagle's.
6 The Lord works righteousness
   and justice for all who are oppressed.
7 He made known his ways to Moses,
   his acts to the people of Israel.
8 The Lord is merciful and gracious,
   slow to anger and abounding in steadfast love.
9 He will not always chide,
   nor will he keep his anger forever.
10 He does not deal with us according to our sins,
   nor repay us according to our iniquities.
11 For as high as the heavens are above the earth,
   so great is his steadfast love toward those who fear him;
12 as far as the east is from the west,
   so far does he remove our transgressions from us.
13 As a father shows compassion to his children,
   so the Lord shows compassion to those who fear him.
14 For he knows our frame;
   he remembers that we are dust.

TUESDAY

Micah 3:1-4

1 And I said:
Hear, you heads of Jacob
  and rulers of the house of Israel!
Is it not for you to know justice?—
2 you who hate the good and love the evil,
who tear the skin from off my people
  and their flesh from off their bones,
3 who eat the flesh of my people,
  and flay their skin from off them,
and break their bones in pieces
  and chop them up like meat in a pot,
  like flesh in a cauldron.
4 Then they will cry to the Lord,
  but he will not answer them;
he will hide his face from them at that time,
  because they have made their deeds evil.

Isaiah 55:8-9

8 For my thoughts are not your thoughts,
  neither are your ways my ways, declares the Lord.
9 For as the heavens are higher than the earth,
  so are my ways higher than your ways
  and my thoughts than your thoughts.

WEDNESDAY

Micah 3:5-8

5 Thus says the Lord concerning the prophets
  who lead my people astray,
who cry "Peace"
  when they have something to eat,
but declare war against him
  who puts nothing into their mouths.
6 Therefore it shall be night to you, without vision,
  and darkness to you, without divination.
The sun shall go down on the prophets,
  and the day shall be black over them;
7 the seers shall be disgraced,
  and the diviners put to shame;
they shall all cover their lips,
  for there is no answer from God.
8 But as for me, I am filled with power,
  with the Spirit of the Lord,
  and with justice and might,
to declare to Jacob his transgression
  and to Israel his sin.

James 5:19-20

19 My brothers, if anyone among you wanders from the truth and someone brings him back, 20 let him know that whoever brings back a sinner from his wandering will save his soul from death and will cover a multitude of sins.

THURSDAY

Micah 3:9-12

9 Hear this, you heads of the house of Jacob
and rulers of the house of Israel,
who detest justice
and make crooked all that is straight,
10 who build Zion with blood
and Jerusalem with iniquity.
11 Its heads give judgment for a bribe;
its priests teach for a price;
its prophets practice divination for money;
yet they lean on the Lord and say,
"Is not the Lord in the midst of us?
No disaster shall come upon us."
12 Therefore because of you
Zion shall be plowed as a field;
Jerusalem shall become a heap of ruins,
and the mountain of the house a wooded height.

Psalm 82

1 God has taken his place in the divine council;
in the midst of the gods he holds judgment:
2 "How long will you judge unjustly
and show partiality to the wicked? Selah
3 Give justice to the weak and the fatherless;
maintain the right of the afflicted and the destitute.
4 Rescue the weak and the needy;
deliver them from the hand of the wicked."
5 They have neither knowledge nor understanding,
they walk about in darkness;
all the foundations of the earth are shaken.
6 I said, "You are gods,
sons of the Most High, all of you;
7 nevertheless, like men you shall die,
and fall like any prince."
8 Arise, O God, judge the earth;
for you shall inherit all the nations!

FRIDAY

Micah 4:1-5

1 It shall come to pass in the latter days
   that the mountain of the house of the Lord
shall be established as the highest of the mountains,
   and it shall be lifted up above the hills;
and peoples shall flow to it,
2   and many nations shall come, and say:
"Come, let us go up to the mountain of the Lord,
   to the house of the God of Jacob,
that he may teach us his ways
   and that we may walk in his paths."
For out of Zion shall go forth the law,
   and the word of the Lord from Jerusalem.
3 He shall judge between many peoples,
   and shall decide disputes for strong nations far away;
and they shall beat their swords into plowshares,
   and their spears into pruning hooks;
nation shall not lift up sword against nation,
   neither shall they learn war anymore;
4 but they shall sit every man under his vine and under his fig tree,
   and no one shall make them afraid,
   for the mouth of the Lord of hosts has spoken.
5 For all the peoples walk
   each in the name of its god,
but we will walk in the name of the Lord our God
   forever and ever.

Revelation 21:1-8

1 Then I saw a new heaven and a new earth, for the first heaven and the first earth had passed away, and the sea was no more. 2 And I saw the holy city, new Jerusalem, coming down out of heaven from God, prepared as a bride adorned for her husband. 3 And I heard a loud voice from the throne saying, "Behold, the dwelling place of God is with man. He will dwell with them, and they will be his people, and God himself will be with them as their God. 4 He will wipe away every tear from their eyes, and death shall be no more, neither shall there be mourning, nor crying, nor pain anymore, for the former things have passed away."

5 And he who was seated on the throne said, "Behold, I am making all things new." Also he said, "Write this down, for these words are trustworthy and true." 6 And he said to me, "It is done! I am the Alpha and the Omega, the beginning and the end. To the thirsty I will give from the spring of the water of life without payment. 7 The one who conquers will have this heritage, and I will be his God and he will be my son. 8 But as for the cowardly, the faithless, the detestable, as for murderers, the sexually immoral, sorcerers, idolaters, and all liars, their portion will be in the lake that burns with fire and sulfur, which is the second death."

MONDAY

Read:
Micah 2:12-13, Psalm 103:1-14

SOAP:
Micah 2:12

1. Write out today's **SCRIPTURE** passage.

2. On the blank page to the right, **DRAW** or **WRITE** what this passage means to you.

3. My **PRAYER** for today:

TUESDAY

Read:
Micah 3:1-4, Isaiah 55:8-9

SOAP:
Isaiah 55:8-9

1. Write out today's **SCRIPTURE** passage.

2. On the blank page to the right, **DRAW** or **WRITE** what this passage means to you.

3. My **PRAYER** for today:

WEDNESDAY

Read:
Micah 3:5-8, James 5:19-20

SOAP:
Micah 3:8

1. Write out today's **SCRIPTURE** passage.

2. On the blank page to the right, **DRAW** or **WRITE** what this passage means to you.

3. My **PRAYER** for today:

THURSDAY

Read:
Micah 3:9-12, Psalm 82

SOAP:
Psalm 82:8

1. Write out today's **SCRIPTURE** passage.

2. On the blank page to the right, **DRAW** or **WRITE** what this passage means to you.

3. My **PRAYER** for today:

FRIDAY

Read:

Micah 4:1-5, Revelation 21:1-8

SOAP:

Micah 4:5

1. Write out today's **SCRIPTURE** passage.

2. On the blank page to the right, **DRAW** or **WRITE** what this passage means to you.

3. My **PRAYER** for today:

THIS WEEK I LEARNED...

USE THE SPACE BELOW TO DRAW A PICTURE OR WRITE ABOUT WHAT YOU LEARNED THIS WEEK FROM YOUR TIME IN GOD'S WORD.

PRAYER

WRITE DOWN YOUR PRAYER REQUESTS AND PRAISES FOR EACH DAY.

Prayer focus for this week:
Spend time praying for your friends.

MONDAY

TUESDAY

WEDNESDAY

THURSDAY

FRIDAY

WEEK 3

And he shall stand and
shepherd his flock in the
strength of the Lord,
in the majesty of the
name of the Lord his God.
And they shall dwell secure,
for now he shall be great
to the ends of the earth.
And he shall be their peace.

Micah 5:4-5a

SCRIPTURE FOR WEEK 3

MONDAY

Micah 4:6-8

6 In that day, declares the Lord,
I will assemble the lame
and gather those who have been driven away
and those whom I have afflicted;
7 and the lame I will make the remnant,
and those who were cast off, a strong nation;
and the Lord will reign over them in Mount Zion
from this time forth and forevermore.
8 And you, O tower of the flock,
hill of the daughter of Zion,
to you shall it come,
the former dominion shall come,
kingship for the daughter of Jerusalem.

Psalm 93

1 The Lord reigns; he is robed in majesty;
the Lord is robed; he has put on strength as his belt.
Yes, the world is established; it shall never be moved.
2 Your throne is established from of old;
you are from everlasting.
3 The floods have lifted up, O Lord,
the floods have lifted up their voice;
the floods lift up their roaring.
4 Mightier than the thunders of many waters,
mightier than the waves of the sea,
the Lord on high is mighty!
5 Your decrees are very trustworthy;
holiness befits your house,
O Lord, forevermore.

TUESDAY

Micah 4:9-13

9 Now why do you cry aloud?
Is there no king in you?
Has your counselor perished,
that pain seized you like a woman in labor?
10 Writhe and groan, O daughter of Zion,
like a woman in labor,
for now you shall go out from the city
and dwell in the open country;
you shall go to Babylon.
There you shall be rescued;

there the Lord will redeem you
from the hand of your enemies.
11 Now many nations
are assembled against you,
saying, "Let her be defiled,
and let our eyes gaze upon Zion."
12 But they do not know
the thoughts of the Lord;
they do not understand his plan,
that he has gathered them as sheaves to the threshing floor.
13 Arise and thresh,
O daughter of Zion,
for I will make your horn iron,
and I will make your hoofs bronze;
you shall beat in pieces many peoples;
and shall devote their gain to the Lord,
their wealth to the Lord of the whole earth.

Romans 8:28

28 And we know that for those who love God all things work together for good, for those who are called according to his purpose.

WEDNESDAY

Micah 5:1-6

1 Now muster your troops, O daughter of troops;
siege is laid against us;
with a rod they strike the judge of Israel
on the cheek.
2 But you, O Bethlehem Ephrathah,
who are too little to be among the clans of Judah,
from you shall come forth for me
one who is to be ruler in Israel,
whose coming forth is from of old,
from ancient days.
3 Therefore he shall give them up until the time
when she who is in labor has given birth;
then the rest of his brothers shall return
to the people of Israel.
4 And he shall stand and shepherd his flock in the strength of the Lord,
in the majesty of the name of the Lord his God.
And they shall dwell secure, for now he shall be great
to the ends of the earth.
5 And he shall be their peace.
When the Assyrian comes into our land
and treads in our palaces,
then we will raise against him seven shepherds
and eight princes of men;
6 they shall shepherd the land of Assyria with the sword,

and the land of Nimrod at its entrances;
and he shall deliver us from the Assyrian
when he comes into our land
and treads within our border.

2 Chronicles 32:20-23

20 Then Hezekiah the king and Isaiah the prophet, the son of Amoz, prayed because of this and cried to heaven. 21 And the Lord sent an angel, who cut off all the mighty warriors and commanders and officers in the camp of the king of Assyria. So he returned with shame of face to his own land. And when he came into the house of his god, some of his own sons struck him down there with the sword. 22 So the Lord saved Hezekiah and the inhabitants of Jerusalem from the hand of Sennacherib king of Assyria and from the hand of all his enemies, and he provided for them on every side. 23 And many brought gifts to the Lord to Jerusalem and precious things to Hezekiah king of Judah, so that he was exalted in the sight of all nations from that time onward.

For Further Reading: 2 Chronicles 32

THURSDAY

Micah 5:7-9

7 Then the remnant of Jacob shall be
in the midst of many peoples
like dew from the Lord,
like showers on the grass,
which delay not for a man
nor wait for the children of man.
8 And the remnant of Jacob shall be among the nations,
in the midst of many peoples,
like a lion among the beasts of the forest,
like a young lion among the flocks of sheep,
which, when it goes through, treads down
and tears in pieces, and there is none to deliver.
9 Your hand shall be lifted up over your adversaries,
and all your enemies shall be cut off.

Acts 17:1-4

1 Now when they had passed through Amphipolis and Apollonia, they came to Thessalonica, where there was a synagogue of the Jews. 2 And Paul went in, as was his custom, and on three Sabbath days he reasoned with them from the Scriptures, 3 explaining and proving that it was necessary for the Christ to suffer and to rise from the dead, and saying, "This Jesus, whom I proclaim to you, is the Christ." 4 And some of them were persuaded and joined Paul and Silas, as did a great many of the devout Greeks and not a few of the leading women.

Acts 18:1-4, 24

1 After this Paul left Athens and went to Corinth. 2 And he found a Jew named Aquila, a native of Pontus, recently come from Italy with his wife Priscilla, because Claudius had commanded all the Jews to leave Rome. And he went to see them,3 and because he was of

the same trade he stayed with them and worked, for they were tentmakers by trade. 4 And he reasoned in the synagogue every Sabbath, and tried to persuade Jews and Greeks.

24 Now a Jew named Apollos, a native of Alexandria, came to Ephesus. He was an eloquent man, competent in the Scriptures.

For Further Reading: Acts 17, 18, 19

FRIDAY

Micah 5:10-15

10 And in that day, declares the Lord,
I will cut off your horses from among you
and will destroy your chariots;
11 and I will cut off the cities of your land
and throw down all your strongholds;
12 and I will cut off sorceries from your hand,
and you shall have no more tellers of fortunes;
13 and I will cut off your carved images
and your pillars from among you,
and you shall bow down no more
to the work of your hands;
14 and I will root out your Asherah images from among you
and destroy your cities.
15 And in anger and wrath I will execute vengeance
on the nations that did not obey.

Psalm 50:15-23

15 and call upon me in the day of trouble;
I will deliver you, and you shall glorify me."
16 But to the wicked God says:
"What right have you to recite my statutes
or take my covenant on your lips?
17 For you hate discipline,
and you cast my words behind you.
18 If you see a thief, you are pleased with him,
and you keep company with adulterers.
19 "You give your mouth free rein for evil,
and your tongue frames deceit.
20 You sit and speak against your brother;
you slander your own mother's son.
21 These things you have done, and I have been silent;
you thought that I was one like yourself.
But now I rebuke you and lay the charge before you.
22 "Mark this, then, you who forget God,
lest I tear you apart, and there be none to deliver!
23 The one who offers thanksgiving as his sacrifice glorifies me;
to one who orders his way rightly
I will show the salvation of God!"

MONDAY

Read:
Micah 4:6-8, Psalm 93

SOAP:
Micah 4:7

1. Write out today's **SCRIPTURE** passage.

2. On the blank page to the right, **DRAW** or **WRITE** what this passage means to you.

3. My **PRAYER** for today:

TUESDAY

Read:
Micah 4:9-13, Romans 8:28

SOAP:
Micah 4:12

1. Write out today's SCRIPTURE passage.

2. On the blank page to the right, DRAW or WRITE what this passage means to you.

3. My PRAYER for today:

WEDNESDAY

Read:
Micah 5:1-6, 2 Chronicles 32:20-23

SOAP:
Micah 5:4-5a

1. Write out today's **SCRIPTURE** passage.

2. On the blank page to the right, **DRAW** or **WRITE** what this passage means to you.

3. My **PRAYER** for today:

THURSDAY

Read:
Micah 5:7-9, Acts 17:1-4; 18:1-4, 24

SOAP:
Micah 5:7

1. Write out today's **SCRIPTURE** passage.

2. On the blank page to the right, **DRAW** or **WRITE** what this passage means to you.

3. My **PRAYER** for today:

FRIDAY

Read:
Micah 5:10-15, Psalm 50:15-23

SOAP:
Micah 5:15

1. Write out today's **SCRIPTURE** passage.

2. On the blank page to the right, **DRAW** or **WRITE** what this passage means to you.

3. My **PRAYER** for today:

THIS WEEK I LEARNED...

USE THE SPACE BELOW TO DRAW A PICTURE OR WRITE ABOUT WHAT YOU LEARNED THIS WEEK FROM YOUR TIME IN GOD'S WORD.

PRAYER

WRITE DOWN YOUR PRAYER REQUESTS AND PRAISES FOR EACH DAY.

Prayer focus for this week:
Spend time praying for your church.

MONDAY

TUESDAY

WEDNESDAY

THURSDAY

FRIDAY

WEEK 4

He has told you,
O man, what is good;
and what does the Lord
require of you
but to do justice,
and to love kindness,
and to walk humbly
with your God?

Micah 6:8

SCRIPTURE FOR WEEK 4

MONDAY

Micah 6:1-8

1 Hear what the Lord says:
Arise, plead your case before the mountains,
  and let the hills hear your voice.
2 Hear, you mountains, the indictment of the Lord,
  and you enduring foundations of the earth,
for the Lord has an indictment against his people,
  and he will contend with Israel.
3 "O my people, what have I done to you?
  How have I wearied you? Answer me!
4 For I brought you up from the land of Egypt
  and redeemed you from the house of slavery,
and I sent before you Moses,
  Aaron, and Miriam.
5 O my people, remember what Balak king of Moab devised,
  and what Balaam the son of Beor answered him,
and what happened from Shittim to Gilgal,
  that you may know the righteous acts of the Lord."
6 "With what shall I come before the Lord,
  and bow myself before God on high?
Shall I come before him with burnt offerings,
  with calves a year old?
7 Will the Lord be pleased with thousands of rams,
  with ten thousands of rivers of oil?
Shall I give my firstborn for my transgression,
  the fruit of my body for the sin of my soul?"
8 He has told you, O man, what is good;
  and what does the Lord require of you
but to do justice, and to love kindness,
  and to walk humbly with your God?

Galatians 4:12-16

12 Brothers, I entreat you, become as I am, for I also have become as you are. You did me no wrong. 13 You know it was because of a bodily ailment that I preached the gospel to you at first, 14 and though my condition was a trial to you, you did not scorn or despise me, but received me as an angel of God, as Christ Jesus. 15 What then has become of your blessedness? For I testify to you that, if possible, you would have gouged out your eyes and given them to me. 16 Have I then become your enemy by telling you the truth?

TUESDAY

Micah 6:9-15

9 The voice of the Lord cries to the city—
and it is sound wisdom to fear your name:
"Hear of the rod and of him who appointed it!
10 Can I forget any longer the treasures of wickedness in the house of the wicked,
and the scant measure that is accursed?
11 Shall I acquit the man with wicked scales
and with a bag of deceitful weights?
12 Your rich men are full of violence;
your inhabitants speak lies,
and their tongue is deceitful in their mouth.
13 Therefore I strike you with a grievous blow,
making you desolate because of your sins.
14 You shall eat, but not be satisfied,
and there shall be hunger within you;
you shall put away, but not preserve,
and what you preserve I will give to the sword.
15 You shall sow, but not reap;
you shall tread olives, but not anoint yourselves with oil;
you shall tread grapes, but not drink wine.

Job 40:1-9

1 And the Lord said to Job:
2 "Shall a faultfinder contend with the Almighty?
He who argues with God, let him answer it."
3 Then Job answered the Lord and said:
4 "Behold, I am of small account; what shall I answer you?
I lay my hand on my mouth.
5 I have spoken once, and I will not answer;
twice, but I will proceed no further."
6 Then the Lord answered Job out of the whirlwind and said:
7 "Dress for action like a man;
I will question you, and you make it known to me.
8 Will you even put me in the wrong?
Will you condemn me that you may be in the right?
9 Have you an arm like God,
and can you thunder with a voice like his?

WEDNESDAY

Micah 7:1-7

1 Woe is me! For I have become
as when the summer fruit has been gathered,
as when the grapes have been gleaned:

there is no cluster to eat,
  no first-ripe fig that my soul desires.
2 The godly has perished from the earth,
  and there is no one upright among mankind;
they all lie in wait for blood,
  and each hunts the other with a net.
3 Their hands are on what is evil, to do it well;
  the prince and the judge ask for a bribe,
and the great man utters the evil desire of his soul;
  thus they weave it together.
4 The best of them is like a brier,
  the most upright of them a thorn hedge.
The day of your watchmen, of your punishment, has come;
  now their confusion is at hand.
5 Put no trust in a neighbor;
  have no confidence in a friend;
guard the doors of your mouth
  from her who lies in your arms;
6 for the son treats the father with contempt,
  the daughter rises up against her mother,
the daughter-in-law against her mother-in-law;
  a man's enemies are the men of his own house.
7 But as for me, I will look to the Lord;
  I will wait for the God of my salvation;
  my God will hear me.

THURSDAY

Micah 7:8-13

8 Rejoice not over me, O my enemy;
  when I fall, I shall rise;
when I sit in darkness,
  the Lord will be a light to me.
9 I will bear the indignation of the Lord
  because I have sinned against him,
until he pleads my cause
  and executes judgment for me.
He will bring me out to the light;
  I shall look upon his vindication.
10 Then my enemy will see,
  and shame will cover her who said to me,
  "Where is the Lord your God?"
My eyes will look upon her;
  now she will be trampled down
  like the mire of the streets.
11 A day for the building of your walls!
  In that day the boundary shall be far extended.

12 In that day they will come to you,
from Assyria and the cities of Egypt,
and from Egypt to the River,
from sea to sea and from mountain to mountain.
13 But the earth will be desolate
because of its inhabitants,
for the fruit of their deeds.

FRIDAY

Micah 7:14-20

14 Shepherd your people with your staff,
the flock of your inheritance,
who dwell alone in a forest
in the midst of a garden land;
let them graze in Bashan and Gilead
as in the days of old.
15 As in the days when you came out of the land of Egypt,
I will show them marvelous things.
16 The nations shall see and be ashamed of all their might;
they shall lay their hands on their mouths;
their ears shall be deaf;
17 they shall lick the dust like a serpent,
like the crawling things of the earth;
they shall come trembling out of their strongholds;
they shall turn in dread to the Lord our God,
and they shall be in fear of you.
18 Who is a God like you, pardoning iniquity
and passing over transgression
for the remnant of his inheritance?
He does not retain his anger forever,
because he delights in steadfast love.
19 He will again have compassion on us;
he will tread our iniquities underfoot.
You will cast all our sins
into the depths of the sea.
20 You will show faithfulness to Jacob
and steadfast love to Abraham,
as you have sworn to our fathers
from the days of old.

MONDAY

Read:
Micah 6:1-8, Galatians 4:12-16

SOAP:
Micah 6:8

1. Write out today's **SCRIPTURE** passage.

2. On the blank page to the right, **DRAW** or **WRITE** what this passage means to you.

3. My **PRAYER** for today:

TUESDAY

Read:
Micah 6:9-15, Job 40:1-9

SOAP:
Job 40:8-9

1. Write out today's **SCRIPTURE** passage.

2. On the blank page to the right, **DRAW** or **WRITE** what this passage means to you.

3. My **PRAYER** for today:

WEDNESDAY

Read:
Micah 7:1-7

SOAP:
Micah 7:7

1. Write out today's **SCRIPTURE** passage.

2. On the blank page to the right, **DRAW** or **WRITE** what this passage means to you.

3. My **PRAYER** for today:

THURSDAY

Read:
Micah 7:8-13

SOAP:
Micah 7:8-9

1. Write out today's SCRIPTURE passage.

2. On the blank page to the right, DRAW or WRITE what this passage means to you.

3. My PRAYER for today:

FRIDAY

Read:
Micah 7:14-20

SOAP:
Micah 7:18-20

1. Write out today's **SCRIPTURE** passage.

2. On the blank page to the right, **DRAW** or **WRITE** what this passage means to you.

3. My **PRAYER** for today:

THIS WEEK I LEARNED...

USE THE SPACE BELOW TO DRAW A PICTURE OR WRITE ABOUT WHAT YOU LEARNED THIS WEEK FROM YOUR TIME IN GOD'S WORD.

Made in the USA
Coppell, TX
30 March 2022